PRAYER

IN THE

FAMILY

by John and Beth Viatori

*All booklets are published thanks to the
generous support of the members of the
Catholic Truth Society*

CATHOLIC TRUTH SOCIETY
PUBLISHERS TO THE HOLY SEE

CONTENTS

THE NECESSITY OF PRAYER

Many people experience a certain shyness with respect to prayer. But we have a God whose most urgent wish is that we should share his life and know his love. It is to answer this welcome, that we engage in prayer.

The *Catechism of the Catholic Church* defines prayer as the "vital and personal relationship with the living and true God" (2558). Like any relationship, prayer depends on communication and time spent in each other's company.

One's relationship with God is as delicate and unique as any relationship in one's life, while being more important because, unlike other relationships, it touches every aspect of our lives and encompasses the goal and end of our lives. When seen in this light, it becomes clear that our life's very meaning depends upon what St. Teresa of Avila called "taking time frequently to be with Him whom we know loves us" - that is, taking time for prayer.

Why should we pray in the family?

Our children are our treasures. Yet we parents must remind ourselves that these treasures that were entrusted to us, were made by God for his love. In the famous words of Saint Augustine, "You have made us for yourself, Lord, and our hearts are restless until they rest in you." Though we want to give our children everything good, no quantity of good things that we give them can satisfy the longing for God that is planted in their hearts. We may have already seen this restlessness in our children. We may have seen them searching for happiness, pleasure, meaning or belonging. This seeking can only be answered by the Love that created them for itself. We want them to know this Love, to have the consolation of God's presence throughout their lives and to spend eternity in the company of Him and all their loved ones.

Prayer is more than an earthly investment whose benefits we will reap for all eternity. Bringing up our children in prayer means introducing them into God's company, at this very moment as well as forever. "The life of prayer is the habit of being in the presence of the thrice-holy God and in communion with him" (*CCC* 2565). By training us to live in the presence of God and in communion with him, prayer gives us a foretaste of heaven now. It is the key to a life lived in vibrant faith, a life spent in awareness of the fact that God is constantly with us, managing everything for our good. God is offering us his friendship and a share in his life right now, which we can enjoy by integrating prayer more into our daily lives.

Since no human being has the ability to relate to God as one friend relates to another without a special gift from God, Christian prayer is made possible by the sanctifying grace that is first given through baptism.

Jesus said, "Let the little children come to me, and do not hinder them; for the kingdom of God belongs to such as them" (*Mt* 19:14). Because of their baptism, children already carry sanctifying grace - the life of the Trinity - within them. However, children may not be aware of this life and how much God loves them; they rely on their parents to teach them. They are as entitled to a relationship with the God who created and redeemed them as any adult. But this relationship must be cultivated in them at their own level of interaction. To leave the spiritual life of our children undeveloped until they are old enough to seek it for themselves would be to do them a great disservice. It would mean depriving them of the love that every human needs most because they are too small to know where to find it. This is why we want to cultivate prayer in our families.

Christ promised us that wherever two or more gathered in his name, he would be present (*Mt* 18:20). Especially here, where the community is founded on the parents' sacrament of marriage, the Lord is present; through the sacrament, he constantly gives us the supernatural help that we need to live this married life and raise these children well. This is what sacramental grace is - the supernatural help from God to perform the work of the sacrament. Since the work of the sacrament of marriage is raising children in a common life, God gives every Christian marriage the necessary help to do this job well.

The Domestic Church

The Catechism tells us:

> The Christian family is the first place of education
> in prayer. Based on the sacrament of marriage, the
> family is the "domestic church" where God's
> children learn to pray "as the Church" and to
> persevere in prayer. For young children in
> particular, daily family prayer is the first witness of
> the Church's living memory as awakened patiently
> by the Holy Spirit. (*CCC*, 2685)

The family is a "domestic Church" and "the first place
of education in prayer" because it is the first place that
children learn about their faith. The parents are the first
apostles, bringing the message of the Gospel to their
children by their own attitudes and examples as well as
what they explicitly teach their children about God. Like
the Church at large, the family teaches its members to
pray by instructing children both in the devotions and
practices of prayer and by its example of perseverence,
faith, and humility. And just as Christ promised the
Twelve Apostles that the Holy Spirit would never
abandon the Church, but would teach them all things,
parents can depend upon the Spirit's guidance and
instruction as they direct their own little domestic church.

A young mother once asked Luigi Guissani, the late founder of the religious movement Communion and Liberation, what he thought of Maria Montessori. He told her, "She's good, but you don't need a method to raise your children. You just need to show them that Christ is someone who is present now, not something in the past, something that doesn't affect your ordinary life - and you can do this by letting your children see you and your husband pray together. They need to know that they depend on Another - their life is not their own project or plan. And seeing you pray, taking all your needs before the Lord, is also a good example of that."

With this advice, Don Giussani emphasised the greatest good of prayer - that it is the human action most central to loving God. Yet the love of God is also the source of all other loves, a fact that is evident in the secondary effects of prayer. By focusing on God's goodness, praise and adoration take us out of ourselves, reminding us that we are not at the centre of life. Our petitions and requests are practice in trusting God to give us what we need, while prayers of thanksgiving remind us that everything we have, we have received. Prayers of intercession for others are often a very good entry into the life of prayer, for those of us who are shy about praying in front of others. Often even when we can't bring ourselves to go to God in prayer on our own behalf, the needs of our loved ones or acquaintances compel us to pray. Sometimes praying each

Hail Mary of the rosary for a particular intention can help us to concentrate when it is especially difficult to do so. This also allows our love for God and our love for others to reinforce and sustain each other.

We must have no illusions about the delicate nature of introducing (or deepening) prayer in the family. What is at stake is a relationship with God, the greatest good we could hope to hand on to our children. But a living spiritual life is by its very nature out of our power to give. A relationship with God can neither be forced nor taught. We can work to establish the conditions in which this relationship can thrive; we can set it forth as something to be desired by our own examples; and we can personally pray for our loved ones to grow in the love of God.

Yet neither should we grow discouraged at the task that we have as parents. God never asks the impossible, and that we and our children should grow in love of him and each other is his dearest desire for us. God guides and teaches us through everything we experience: every moment of every day, and every circumstance of our lives are directed by him. We can depend upon his unfailing help in the enterprise of marriage; as he promised to guide and teach the Church, so we can expect our own domestic churches to be led and taught by the Holy Spirit. This way we can strive toward our goal of enjoying family prayer as time spent together in the company of the ones we love most in the world - our family and our Lord.

PERSONAL PRAYER IS THE FOUNDATION
FOR FAMILY PRAYER

The Catechism of the Catholic Church describes the duty that faces parents in these terms:

> The catechesis of children, young people, and adults aims at teaching them to *meditate on The Word of God in personal prayer, practising it in liturgical prayer, and internalising it at all times in order to bear fruit in a new life.* (*CCC*, 2688)

Our responsibility for teaching our children the faith falls into three tasks: we must help them learn to meditate on the Word of God in personal prayer, practise it in liturgical prayer, and internalise it such that it transforms their lives. The "Word of God" intended here does not merely refer to the Bible, but to the Son of God whom those Scriptures were written in order to proclaim. He is the Word who was from the beginning with God, who is God become flesh so that those who believe in him might have eternal life (Cf. *Jn* 1:1-18; 3:16-21). This is the challenge of catechesis: to teach our children how to unite themselves with the Word in personal prayer, liturgy, and everyday life. Accordingly, we will first explore the elements of personal prayer before discussing the liturgical practices that can take place in a family, and ways that the family can live prayer in its daily life.

Teaching our children to engage in personal prayer is no easy task. Many of us are still trying to learn how to develop personal prayer ourselves. How can we possibly instruct other people in something so intimate, so *personal?* Yet our discussion of family prayer must begin with personal prayer, because a family is made up of persons, each called by God, each on his own individual journey toward truth and love. A family's prayer life stands or falls with the personal spiritual lives of the individual family members. As parents, we cannot establish a relationship with God in our children or train them to turn to him. However, we can adopt practices that will provide the conditions for our children to "meditate on the Word of God." We can provide them with an example of praying with faith, humility, and perseverence, and we can teach them prayers that will unfold in their understanding as they grow.

As is the case with any community, family prayer is only as good as the prayer of its members. For a family to pray well together, the members must be praying well individually. This means that the first step and the constant wellspring for deepening and enriching family prayer is to deepen and enrich one's own spiritual life. Many of us have an aversion to praying with others because of some experience of communal prayer which seemed to be "all for show." The antidote for this obstacle to prayer in the family is for the family members, especially the parents, to be constantly and honestly at work on their own relationships with God while praying with the family and praying individually. Indeed, the example of a parent who is himself sincerely seeking to pray better teaches children more effectively than anything else. To pray better means striving to pray, as St. Thomas Aquinas teaches, with faith, humility, and perseverance.

Prayer requires faith - The overarching quality that animates our attempts to pray is, of course, faith. Praying with faith means believing that "God exists and he rewards those who seek him" (*Heb* 11:6).

Believing that God exists is more than just acknowledging that there is some more-powerful being who made all of the things we see around us. It means accepting that right here, right now, God is holding all things in existence, and that he intends each good thing to be exactly as it is, and allows each bad thing to be exactly as it is so that he can bring good out of it.

By the same token, to believe that God rewards those who seek him entails more than just recognising that the one who holds the universe in being will provide benefits to those who ask. It means believing that God became man to free us from death, and that the reward he wants to give us is not just material and limited to this life. The reward he wants to give us is himself, here and now, as the downpayment on giving us himself forever.

Prayer requires humility - It may seem a truism that the example of the parents is the most powerful teacher in spiritual matters. Yet this example is only effective when it springs honestly from a sincere interior life on the parent's part. Humility involves admitting, also before our children, that we too are travellers on this journey to greater closeness with God. We have not arrived at a destination that we expect to bring them to, but rather we hope that they will join us in our quest to love better.

We, as parents, must realise that every child (indeed, every person) is being led along this path by the Holy Spirit, and if we try to push children according to our own conceptions, we risk hampering their progress. Talking down to children, oversentimentalising, or attempting to dilute the religious content of what we tell them trivialises the truths we are hoping to communicate. Children of every age are put off prayer by people who exaggerate their religious feeling or talk too much about spiritual things. Even small children can detect the contrived, manipulative quality of this kind of behaviour. Worse yet, if, as parents, our external appearance does not derive authentically from an internal experience, it risks seeming like or even becoming hypocrisy.

The British educator, Susan Schaeffer Macaulay, was raised in the L'Abri religious community founded by her parents. She herself grew to maturity in the Christian faith, yet she has this caveat to give to parents:

All of this is so important that we walk a delicate line. We ourselves need to pray to the Lord for wisdom. We should not overdo our own enthusiasm, or the children will hear too much talk on the matter, and they will be tired of it... There are many ways of applying the "Christianity that is true to the total reality." We don't have to make every day a sort of Sunday school lesson to achieve this. There are several dangers in that sort of approach. Too much pious talk, talk, talk. Too many "holy moments." Expecting continual religious experiences. Not letting children "be." Not letting them wonder, puzzle, and ask... We let the children come to our Lord by letting them know about Him... They can read His words, see that we are all in relationship with Him, that we have a King, Saviour, Helper, Friend. Later on, the *thinking aspects* - the realisation that this is truth - will follow. But don't try to schedule *how* the child will feel, *how* he should react, *when* he should understand each step, etc. Get out of the way. Let the child, God, and His Word be alone together. Let them work out their own relationship.[1]

Another habit that can falsify prayer and lead to rebellion in the children is a parent's use of prayer time as a time to moralise. Here we are not referring to a direct correction of a child whose unruliness makes it impossible for others to pray, but rather the *use* of the prayers themselves to send not-so-subtle messages to the members of the family: "Please help so-and-so to be obedient to his mother" or "Let's think of the times today when we have failed to tell the truth ..." When the words that one says in prayer are actually being directed at one's children or one's spouse, it empties prayer, as a time for being with God, of its essential good. Moreover, the example of the parents is shown to be a sham, since the parents are evidently not talking to God but using Him as an excuse to further their own aims. Regardless of how good these aims may be, they can hardly be as good as the lesson that prayer begins with an honest, humble examination of one's own heart. This lesson can only be shown, it cannot be preached.

---

[1] From *For the Children's Sake* by Susan Schaeffer Macaulay, copyright 1984, pages 95, 101, and 104. Used by permission of Crossway Books, a ministry of Good News Publishers, Wheaton, Illinois 60187. www.crossway.com

Prayer requires perseverence - Every family - indeed, every person - encounters difficulties in personal prayer; but as St. Francis de Sales advised concerning the struggle to pray, "It is a happy condition of this war that as long as we are fighting, we are winning." We must not allow ourselves to be deterred by our inability to pray perfectly. Many of us find that we are distracted, sleepy, or lackadaisical when we say the rosary or attend mass. Yet we must realise that these very challenges have faced *every person* who ever attempted to make a commitment to prayer. The doctors of the Church and indeed any good spiritual director can offer suggestions for how to combat these obstacles to the spiritual life. One of the greatest mistakes we can make is to say, "I can't pray these prayers as well as I'd like, so I'm not going to pray them at all." The effort to pray better is one that we will have to make all our lives - it is in fact the very work of loving better.

Another tendency that can threaten our ability to stick with praying is, ironically, discipline that is too inflexible. While we should strive to persevere in prayer, we shouldn't allow our commitment to prayer to make us rigid. Sometimes overly strict discipline cultivates a relationship of fear rather than love and often ends in the rebellion of the children. When the family rosary is invariably a time of reprimand and punishment, all the members of the family risk losing sight of the fact that this time is set aside for cultivating a relationship with God. It should provide the conditions for furthering and deepening a relationship of love - indeed the most important relationship of love in any person's life. If love of God is authentic, it must cultivate love of neighbour (or family member) and vice versa. Christ said, "If you love me, keep my commandments" (*Jn* 14:15) and "my commandment is this: love one another as I have loved you" (*Jn* 15:12). We defeat the purpose of prayer if we allow anger or harshness to enter into prayer time with our family, because this prayer time is precisely for the sake of greater love for our family members and for God.

It may be said that it can be difficult to enjoy the company of Jesus and the saints with small children present, who cannot sit still or keep quiet. The challenge that faces us is to find the balance that will maintain order without injuring this delicate relationship that is unfolding even in the hearts of the smallest listeners. God made children, and he made them to be the way they are. He does not expect them or us to do the impossible - no one understands better the natural limitations of small children than the One who created them with such a nature!

Despite the many obstacles, persistence in prayer is possible, even for a family with very small children. On the one hand, it requires making prayer a necessary part of one's day like brushing one's teeth; and on the other hand, it means allowing that, as in many things, some days will be better than others.

Unity in family prayer

If the example of one parent's praying with faith, humility and perseverance can so profoundly impress children, the unity of the parents in their approach to prayer speaks volumes to children about prayer's importance and how it should be practised. The attitude of the father toward prayer often sets the tone for all the children, but especially for sons. One Catholic man (soon to be ordained a priest) remembers rebelling against prayer as a teenager. What made the difference for him was seeing his father praying. "I think most guys growing up think it's something that women do. They don't see men down on their knees very regularly. My father is a big 'man's man,' so seeing him praying told me that here was something real, something true." A father who leads the family in prayer is a tacit but convincing sign to children that prayer is not something wishy-washy or soft, but important and powerful. Any child's natural experience of his own human father gives him his first intimation of God's fatherhood, "from whom all fatherhood in heaven and on earth takes its name" (*Ep* 3:15).

Nevertheless, single mothers, or those whose husbands are absent, must hold to the certainty that God is giving them the grace to fulfill the task with which they are faced. He not only knows the particularities of each of our situations, but he actually intends these circumstances as specially designed to give us each a chance to grow. All the eventualities of our lives occur in the providence of God, and his grace is at work all the more where the family is in the greatest need. As St. Paul was told when he asked the Lord to take away the suffering in his own situation, "My grace is sufficient for you, for strength is made perfect in weakness" (2 Co 12:9). Periods of weakness or difficulty in our own lives are often the times when we are being perfected spiritually, because it is then that, in our hardship or sadness, we are driven to "cast all our cares on Christ, who cares for us" (cf. 1 P 5:7). In fact, many people find that it is during the most difficult times or circumstances that their prayer lives have really blossomed. One reason for this is certainly that during hardships we realise more fully our utter dependence on God. These times and situations can produce great fruit if we can continue to trust God and turn to him for help.

Indeed, in some ways the greatest challenge can be said to face those parents whose spouses are present but unenthusiastic or even antagonistic toward prayer. Theirs is the delicate task of cultivating prayer with their children and praying for their spouses in a way that is not off-putting or sanctimonious. The example of St. Monica, whose prayers and life brought about the conversion of her son, St. Augustine, has been the comfort and model for countless families who have navigated these tricky waters through the centuries. St. Rita of Cascia also suffered seventeen years of unhappy marriage, but witnessed her husband's conversion through her own intercession before his death.

The grown children of a man who experienced a deep conversion when they were just on the verge of adolescence shared their family's journey to deeper prayer.

At first, the father's new-found fervour caused a rift between himself and his wife, to the point that the couple separated and were on the brink of divorcing. The husband continued to pray, certain that he could not return to his former life, but heart-broken that his faith might mean the loss of his wife and four children. The answer that he received in prayer was, "Just live your faith but keep your mouth shut." He continued his rosaries, daily Mass, and fasting, but less ostentatiously, and he stopped talking about his faith. Finally his wife was compelled to say to him, "I'm so miserable. I want to know why you are so happy?" She undertook to attend daily Mass over the course of one Lent and found that she was experiencing more peace than she had had in a long time. At the end of Lent she made her first confession in 26 years.

She and her husband ended their separation, yet the mother's conversion continued only as a very, very, gradual change. "Eventually," her daughter related, "she started seeing the effects that prayer was having on us her kids and just decided to choose the good of her kids over her own will. There was so much history with my dad that it was very difficult for him to talk to her. But it was through her kids that she saw that this was important to us and she wanted to know what we were interested in."

This father discovered that talking about his faith to a spouse who was not yet ready actually did more harm to their marital unity and their family's spiritual life. Yet his entire family found the example of his silent commitment to prayer more compelling than any preaching. His son added, "Every night he would leave the house and we knew that he was going to pray his rosary and that we were welcome to join him. We knew he was living this faith even if he wasn't saying anything about it, so it had such a profound effect on us."

Of course, the ideal for which we must strive and pray is the unity of the parents in prayer, for the unity of the family will spring from this primary unity. Many couples have found that making time expressly to pray together has strengthened their unity and deepened their love more than anything else. The religious movement Teams of Our Lady is focused on strengthening one's marriage by endeavouring to pray together regularly as a couple. One couple committed to saying night prayers together after their smallest children were in bed. "The older children are welcome to join us if they like, and sometimes they do, but they all know that we guard this time together quite jealously. And when the children see their parents pray together, they see that prayer isn't just a show that's put on for 'us kids'; it's something that our parents think is important enough to spend their own time on."

Despite the many obvious obstacles and challenges that face us as we try to ensure that our family's prayer is personal, we have a powerful ally in this struggle. God himself is our greatest advocate in our efforts to pray better. He is the father who sees his prodigal children while we are "yet at a distance" and hastens to meet us wherever we are on the road to him, so that he may embrace us (Cf. *Lk* 15:11-24). He is the Consoler who prays within us "with sighs too deep for words," because "we ourselves do not know how to pray as we ought" (*Rm* 8:26). He is the Word, who promised to be with his members wherever they are united in prayer. He knows our diffidence and our compunction, and draws near to us to welcome us into his feast.

THE LITURGY OF THE DOMESTIC CHURCH

The word *liturgy* comes from two Greek words meaning, "the work of the people." Liturgy is public prayer, often with a set form that has been handed down through the ages. Liturgy is the prayer that responds to God's invitation of love in communion with the others whom we love. The public nature of liturgy makes it clearly suited for community prayer, as in a family.

The qualities of personal prayer that we considered in the previous section must always be at the heart of the prayers we pray with our family. But it is not enough for family members to pursue their own private relationships with God in isolation from the other members of this domestic church. Coming together with our families to pray on a regular basis is the fundamental step in teaching our children the necessity of prayer, as well as how to pray. Children thrive on predictable routines. Prayer in common offers the perfect opportunity to instruct our children in the words of prayers which will remain their teachers for their whole lives.

Teaching our children the words of specific prayers is an essential component to our family's spiritual life. Those prayers that have set forms have stood the test of time: their phrasing encapsulates theological truths and their practice can offer the comfort of regularity, which gives so much security to smaller children. The verbal quality of prayer - what the Catechism calls "vocal prayer" - derives from our human nature, which is composed of a soul and a body. God created us this way and has communicated with humankind verbally from the beginning: "Through his Word, God speaks to man. By words, mental or vocal, our prayer takes flesh" (*CCC*, 2700). But the verbal quality of prayer also makes it possible for us to pray together as a community.

> Because it is external and so thoroughly human, vocal prayer is the form of prayer most readily accessible to groups. Even interior prayer, however, cannot neglect vocal prayer. Prayer is internalised to the extent that we become aware of him "to whom we speak;" Thus vocal prayer becomes an initial form of contemplative prayer (*CCC*, 2704).

Our goal as Christians should be to transform our entire lives into prayers. Yet we cannot transform our lives into prayer without *praying*.

> Prayer is the life of the new heart. It ought to animate us at every moment... but we cannot pray "at all times" if we do not pray at specific times, consciously willing it. These are the special times of Christian prayer, both in intensity and duration (*CCC*, 2697).

The Catechism reminds us that it is a fallacy to say "my life is a prayer" as an excuse for not spending time intent on praying. Formal prayer - time set aside for talking to God - is essential to forming the rest of one's life around this relationship. This truth derives from the nature of relationships, which depend upon and crave communication as their lifelines. Mother Teresa's Missionaries of Charity, known throughout the world for their works of love and service to the poorest of the poor, typically dedicate five and a half hours of each day to formal prayer. The contemplative sisters spend most of their day in prayer except for two hours devoted to service in the community. Concerning the time set aside for prayer, Mother Teresa said,

> We have much work to do. Our homes for the sick and dying destitute are full everywhere. And from the time we started having adoration every day, our love for Jesus became more intimate, our love for each other more understanding, our love for the poor more compassionate, and we have double the number of vocations. The time we spend in having our daily audience with God is the most precious part of the whole day.

The sisters find that devoting time regularly to being in the presence of the source of all love is absolutely necessary to fulfilling their mission of love to others.

Sanctifying the day

The necessity of regular prayer has been emphasised in the Judeo-Christian tradition from its beginnings. The Jews considered the most important command in their law to be,

> "Hear O Israel: the Lord our God is one Lord; and you shall love the Lord your God with all your heart, and with all your soul, and with all your might. And these words which I command you this day shall be upon your heart; and you shall teach them diligently to your children, and shall talk of them when you sit in your house, and when you walk by the way, and when you lie down, and when you rise." (*Dt* 6:4)

To keep these words upon our heart or to teach them diligently to our children requires practising them at regular intervals - moments Scripture refers to in terms of sitting, walking, waking up or going to bed.

The fact of human nature is that if we don't form a habit of praying certain formal prayers at certain times, the times that we set aside for prayer will become fewer and fewer. The Christian tradition has found that appointing certain times for certain prayers truly does sanctify the day, weaving periods of worship, however brief, into the pattern of daily life. What follow are a few of the most common prayers that can consecrate certain moments of the day.

Grace at Mealtimes

The word *grace* comes from the Latin word *gratia*, here meaning *thanks* or *gratitude*. Filling one of our most basic needs gives us a good opportunity to recognise the gift of our very existence that God sustains at every moment. Moreover, forming a habit of praying before eating is one of the easiest devotions to incorporate, since we can be sure that we will eat many times a day. Families that practise Grace After Meals often find that this formal conclusion also helps prevent a shared mealtime from disintegrating as each member of the family goes his separate way. Many families also remember the dead at this time, a habit that ensures that their souls will be prayed for frequently, while further reminding the living that our lives are in the hands of God. Although a family might develop many beautiful prayers for before and after eating, the most common can be found at the back of the booklet.

The Angelus

The Angelus developed over the centuries as a sort of layman's answer to the Liturgy of the Hours. In some parts of Europe parish bells still ring at 6 a.m., 12 noon, and 6 p.m. to call all the faithful to stop what they are doing and say this little meditation on the Incarnation.

The verses of the Angelus remind us three times a day of the centre-point of history, the event that sanctified all time forever. Mary's words at the heart of this prayer are a model for our prayer lives, and a reminder to ourselves of the purpose of all prayer: to offer ourselves to Love, as he continually offers himself to us.

Bedtime and morning prayers

Many families find that praying together as a family works best in the evenings before bedtime. At this time of day it is especially good to begin prayers by announcing an examination of conscience, observing a moment of quiet, and making an act of contrition. Learning to withdraw from the clutter of noise and look inward is one of the most fundamental lessons in prayer that we can offer our children, for any kind of prayer experience must begin with recollection. This may also be a good time for the parents to ask forgiveness for particular sins they have committed against the children or each other. While we cannot compel anyone else to seek or grant forgiveness, parents who admit their own failings before entering into prayer will give children an example of how an examination of conscience may bear fruit. It's a very concrete opportunity to make peace with one's neighbour before approaching the altar (cf. *Mt* 5:23-24).

Family evening prayers have traditionally taken the form of petitions such as "Bless so-and-so." Such intercessory prayer is especially helpful for people who are new to praying, as Charles Ryder in Evelyn Waugh's *Brideshead Revisited* is able to pray on behalf of two women he cares about before he even realises if he himself believes in God. It also shifts the focus from asking for things for oneself, as though God were a larger, more powerful Father Christmas. In order to further avoid this danger, one family whose children have a wide range of ages encourage everyone to say 'thank you' to God for something in the day: "We try very hard to teach the children that prayer is not just asking for things."

Some families who find that the children are all scattered in the evenings have made time for prayers immediately following breakfast. A morning offering is a good centrepiece to prayers at the beginning of the day, for setting the tone and the goal of one's day. The guardian angel prayer is appropriate at both times; small children respond especially well to this prayer because of its easy rhyming form and the sense of security and protection it conveys.

The Rosary

Among family devotions the Rosary has long enjoyed pride of place. In his apostolic letter *Rosarium Virginis Mariae*, Pope John Paul II explained the particular suitability of the

Rosary for family prayer by the fact that "the Rosary by its nature is a prayer for peace" (*Rosarium Virginis Mariae*, 40).

The family that prays together stays together. The Holy Rosary, by age-old tradition, has shown itself particularly effective as a prayer which brings the family together. Individual family members, in turning their eyes towards Jesus, also regain the ability to look one another in the eye, to communicate, to show solidarity, to forgive one another and to see their covenant of love renewed in the Spirit of God.

Many of the problems facing contemporary families, especially in economically developed societies, result from their increasing difficulty in communicating. Families seldom come together, and the rare occasions that they do are often taken up with watching television. To return to the recitation of the family rosary means filling daily life with very different images, images of the mystery of salvation: the image of the Redeemer, the image of his most Blessed Mother. The family that recites the rosary together reproduces something of the atmosphere of the household of Nazareth: its members place Jesus at the centre, they share his joys and sorrows, they place their needs and their plans in his hands, they draw from him the hope and strength to go on (*Rosarium Virginis Mariae*, 41).

The Rosary is especially suited to the family because it is a prayer to the Mother of Jesus, the Mother of the Church. The Catechism states that, "Like the beloved disciple we welcome Jesus' mother into our homes, for she has become the mother of all the living. We can pray with and to her." (*CCC*, 2679)

Yet from a more practical perspective, the Rosary does well in family prayer because of the simplicity of its structure. The smallest of children learn the Hail Mary easily through the recitation of a decade; the repetitive rhythm tends to calm and settle children at the end of the day; and the number of "Hail Marys" means that one is almost always given another chance to renew his focus on the prayer.

In his document on the Rosary, John Paul II offered several suggestions for ways to deepen our meditation on the life of Christ in the Rosary. Some of these aids which have proved successful in families include books with a Scripture passage for each mystery. Books or cards with pictures or works of art depicting each mystery give smaller children something to focus on and teach them about the content of the mystery before they can read. Allowing each family member to voice his own intentions before each decade often appeals to older children and teenagers and helps all family members to renew their concentration. Praying each Hail Mary for a separate silent intention can help focus

an individual's attention with greater intensity, by
reminding him of what he is praying for. Many parents
find that the office of distributing rosaries or setting up
a small shrine with candles can be conferred upon the
smallest children, so that they are included in the family
liturgy while still too small to participate in other ways.
Some families enjoy saying the rosary with the children
when the children are already in their beds: this custom
allows the parents to complete the Rosary in relative
calm while the children are lulled to sleep in the
company of the Blessed Mother.

The brother of Saint Gianna Molla, the Italian wife and
mother who died in 1962, described the rosary that their
family prayed together every night:

> After dinner, while Papa smoked his cigar, our
> older sister Amalia, an able pianist, played for us
> beautiful sonatas by Chopin, Bach, and Beethoven.
> Then came another important moment in the life of
> our family: the recitation of the Holy Rosary. Papa
> stood before the image of Our Lady with the older
> children while we younger ones were around
> Mamma, who helped us to answer until we fell
> asleep leaning on her knees.[2]

---

[2] From *Saint Gianna Molla: Wife, Mother, Doctor* by Pietro Molla and
Elio Guerriero, published by Ignatius Press, San Francisco. Used with
permission.

The Liturgy of the Hours

Often called "the Breviary" or "the Divine Office," this devotion consists of a cycle of Psalms and short readings from Scripture to be prayed every three hours throughout the day. Praying the Liturgy of the Hours has been one of the duties required of priests and religious for centuries because it is so effective for returning one's mind and heart to God over the course of the day. Praying the psalms is one of the oldest ways of embarking on a life of prayer. Their themes express the most basic experiences of the human condition in dialogue with God: mercy and sinfulness, faith and desolation, suffering and joy. Whether one is learning to pray (or learning again to pray) or deeply formed in habits of prayer, the psalms recall each of us to the fundamental aspects of our relationship with God.

However, to sit down and read 150 psalms may seem an overwhelming task. The Liturgy of the Hours structures the psalms so that they may be *prayed* rather than *read;* their call-and-response format makes them ideal for praying in a community. Families may have greater success with the abbreviated form of the Divine Office called *Shorter Christian Prayer*, or *Shorter Morning and Evening Prayer*. Its length makes it more feasible for children while still introducing families to the rhythm and basic structure of the Liturgy of the Hours.

One couple of our acquaintance, whose attempts at implementing a family rosary had met with sullen resistance for years, had a surprising experience when the mother obtained a subscription to a monthly magazine containing a shorter version of morning and evening prayer for each day. The parents began praying morning and evening prayer together and soon the teenage sons were literally demanding to be allowed to join in. Perhaps two factors were significant in the success of these prayers. First, the fact that the prayers were prescribed in a monthly magazine gave them an authority separate from the parents - it was a prayer which the whole family received, rather than one that the parents dictated to the children. Secondly, the parents were saying prayers together and the teenagers volunteered to take part. This element again removed the sense that the prayers were imposed; it allowed the sons to see the time spent in communal prayer as a pleasant time that they could share with their parents.

When we approach the idea of leading our families into a life of prayer, it may be helpful to remember how the Holy Spirit has led people into relationship with God from the beginning. God addressed the Jewish people directly and with words, and He still enters the hearts of individuals through words. St. Augustine's conversion occurred when he overheard a children's song whose refrain was "pick up and read." He picked up the

Scriptures and encountered directly the God who had been working in his life in many ways all along. His conversion story resembles many modern ones in which God touches someone's heart through the words of a specific prayer or sentence. This is one reason behind the time-tested practice of memorising prayers. Learning certain prayers or passages by heart gives God an entryway into the human mind, so that in a certain way, the answers are already within a person, ready to rise to the surface when he begins to ask the questions.

Sanctifying the Year

The Tradition of the Church proposes to the faithful certain rhythms of praying intended to nourish continual prayer. Some are daily, such as morning and evening prayer, grace before and after meals, the Liturgy of the Hours. Sundays, centred on the Eucharist, are kept holy primarily by prayer. The cycle of the liturgical year and its great feasts are also basic rhythms of the Christian's life of prayer (*CCC*, 2698).

The liturgical year is the unifying structure in which the Christian life of prayer unfolds. It is based on God's activities in creation and redemption: Sunday becomes our day of rest and a celebration of his resurrection; Friday becomes a day of penitence in memory of Christ's passion; the months mark the cycle of natural creation while the liturgical seasons recall our justification by Christ's life and death.

By developing rich traditions to mark the liturgical year a family can render its prayer life ever more beautiful and attractive to its members. The days of the week take on deeper meaning when our minds are called back to the seven days of creation and the three days of the Triduum. Canon Law reminds us that "all Christians are bound in their own way to do penance" on Fridays in commemoration of the suffering that Christ underwent for us. The typical penitential reminder to us of what Christ suffered is to abstain from meat on Fridays. When this action is not possible (or not a sacrifice), some other sacrifice can be substituted. Some people give up sweets on Fridays, or fast on bread and water. Others do more interior acts of penance, such as praying the Stations of the Cross.

As for Sundays, this day of rest and celebration offers the family special chances to spend time together. Although in our culture little remains to distinguish Sunday from any other day of the week, we can distinguish it in our own practices at home. All Catholics are bound to attend Mass every Sunday in order to be reminded at least once a week of the astounding miracle of Christ's Resurrection, and to benefit from its extraordinary graces. For centuries families have set this day apart with a special meal, which forms the natural high-point of the family's week as Sunday Mass forms its spiritual high-point. If the meal is cooked by members of the family who don't normally do the cooking, it can add to the fun for them while providing a day of rest for the usual cooks.

Sunday is the obvious day for families to enjoy time together, by going for a walk together, listening to music together, reading aloud from a story that the whole family can enjoy, or making some special treats together. St. Thérèse of Lisieux remembered fondly the Sundays of her childhood, not only for the highest spiritual reasons, but because those days were set apart by hot chocolate in bed, a pretty dress for Mass, and her father's reading poetry aloud to the whole family gathered together.

The liturgical seasons of Lent and Advent offer many possibilities for family customs that capture the imaginations of small children while teaching them about the coming feast. Advent calendars with little doors to open every day help small children to understand the notion of preparation while making visible the progress toward Christmas. Some families do "Jesse trees" during Advent: each day an Old Testament prophecy about the Saviour is read while an accompanying symbol is hung on a dead branch or colored on a poster. In our family, children enjoyed marking every good deed with a piece of straw to soften the manger (during Advent) or with a crepe-paper rose (during Lent); the activity of *making something* for Jesus seemed to give the children a sense of personal involvement in the time of preparation. Saying daily prayers around an Advent wreath, or doing the Stations of the Cross during Lent are practices that speak to older children as well.

As the family's spiritual life grows, the special seasons of the Church present the clearest opportunities for deepening family prayers. During the penitential seasons of preparation a family might commit to more intense practices, such as night-time prayer vigils, or the old Advent custom of rising earlier for Mass before dawn. During the octave, or eight days, following the feast of All Saints (November 1), the family might make daily visits to a cemetery to say a brief prayer for the dead.

Observing the feast days of family and national saints increases the sense of being a part of the communion of saints. Celebrating family feasts need not be expensive. One little girl of our acquaintance told us, "On the feast of a family saint, whoever's saint it is gets a book and gets to choose what we have for dinner." In another family a child told his brother, "The difference between a birthday and a name day is that on a name day you have a cake, but on a birthday you have a cake and presents." By little gestures like these a family can develop its own liturgical calendar, making the events of the liturgical year personalised and vivid.

The events that a family go through can shape its liturgical life in other ways too. The Roman Missal contains special blessings for a pregnant woman or for a sick child; these can be given by any parish priest. During periods of special difficulty or for a particular need family members might do a novena, in which extra prayers or devotions are adopted for a set time. Special acts of penitence or fasting for heightened family needs are particularly effective, for as Christ told his disciples, certain demons "cannot be driven out by anything but prayer and fasting" (*Mk* 9:29).

There are also daily opportunities to weave more prayer into the fabric of ordinary life. If, for example, every time a person washes his hands, he utters a small prayer for forgiveness, for growth in a particular virtue or for a certain intention, it will add up to many moments devoted to prayer in the course of the day. Any car ride longer than fifteen minutes affords the opportunity to pray the rosary. One mother found that saying, "Behold the handmaid of the Lord," every time she rose during the night to attend to the baby both helped her to perform the task more cheerfully and reminded her of how she was called to serve Jesus in his little ones.

PRAYING WITH OUR WHOLE LIFE

As necessary as it is to set aside time for prayer regularly, this should not imply a division between those moments dedicated to prayer and the rest of the moments in our day. As we stated at the beginning of this booklet, prayer is placing oneself in the presence of God - or rather reminding oneself that we are already at all times in his presence. This is the truth that lies behind the New Testament commandment to "pray without ceasing" (1 *Th* 5:17).

It *is* possible to pray incessantly, even for a family living in the world. It involves allowing all the things that we encounter in the course of the day to remind us of God's presence and draw us into union with him. The Fathers of the Church refer to the "Book of Nature" as the other "book" of God's self-revelation. They did this because the good things of the world cannot help but speak to the soul about the world's creator. This experience is not so uncommon: St. Paul tells us that "ever since the creation of the world, God's eternal power and divine nature, although they are invisible, have been clearly seen and understood through the things that are made" (*Rm* 1:20).

God's presence in the world is palpable for those who look for it; it flames out from the most surprising vessels. Truly we have all had experiences, or known of experiences, in which God has touched the human heart through the glories of nature - like the ocean, or a sunset - or the beauties of human artwork, like the *Pietá* or a piece of music.

It should not surprise us that it should happen this way. God told us from the beginning that everything he created was good; meanwhile he created us with bodies and souls so that we could enjoy the beauty of natural things and think about their meaning. Throughout the Old Testament God was preparing human hearts for his direct revelation by "hinting" about himself through natural things - shepherds and lambs, wine and water, mountains and manna. Then, at the Incarnation, the value of natural things became even greater, when, in a way, God imself became a natural thing, assuming a created human nature and all the limits that a created nature brings. Jesus allowed himself to be limited by place and time; he suffered hunger and thirst and sickness; he made friends and wore clothes, he prayed and celebrated, he was born and he died, like any human being. And because he was God all the time that he was in the world, he changed the importance of natural things by his contact with them. Place and time will never be the same again: now we measure years from His birth, and seasons by Advent,

Lent, and Easter, and days by remembering the moments
of his life. The needs of our body are sanctified by the
fact that Christ had a body: now every time we eat
together, we bless ourselves and the food; we remember
the Last Supper and every time Jesus ate with His family
and his disciples.

The sacraments

The sacraments are a constant reminder in our lives of
the meaning and even the holiness of natural things,
because in each sacrament a natural thing is the basis for
our meeting with the Trinity. The natural act of washing
with water is the basis, the *matter*, for the sacrament of
baptism. But washing in water will not take away
anyone's sins unless it is combined with the words of
Christ, *"I baptise you in the name of the Father and the
Son and the Holy Spirit."* With all the other sacraments
it is the same: the natural thing that is the matter of the
sacrament is transformed by the prayer of the Church, so
that it no longer possesses only natural effects, but
supernatural effects. As part of a sacrament, a natural
thing - like bread and wine, or oil, or even like a man
and a woman spending their lives together - becomes a
way to holiness and the path that the Trinity takes to
enter our souls. This fact should give us an even greater
respect for those natural things that can become God-
bearers in sacraments - and it does! In Slovak

households, for example, ordinary bread is treated with extraordinary love and reverence, because it is the object by which Jesus chose to remain present on earth. It should not be surprising that God makes himself in some way dependent on these simple, humble, ordinary things in order to reach us. That is what he did in the Incarnation of Christ: he became a simple, humble, ordinary thing so that we could see him and touch him and hear his voice. And his eternal power and divine nature were clearly seen through his created human nature, as they are also understood through the things that he has made in the sacraments.

What this means for us as families is that we should endeavour to lead lives with the sacraments at their centre. Because sacraments are sensible signs, they speak to children long before children are capable of understanding their catechism. Moreover, the fact that sacraments follow the course of natural life from birth to death means that families often have the opportunity to witness more of the seven sacraments than single lay people or even religious. Treating the first reception of these sacraments as milestones in the lives of our children will convey somewhat their importance as moments of greatest unity with the Trinity. A baptism should be celebrated as much as a birth, for that is what it is, a birth of a higher order. Saint Gianna Molla honoured the baptismal day of each of her children by having the child

consecrated to Our Lady of Good Counsel on that day.
(The Roman Missal includes prayers of consecration to
the Sacred Heart of Jesus as well as to Our Lady under
many different titles.) The beauty of baptism can be
further savoured by commemorating the anniversary of
family members' baptismal days. One family we know
has asked godparents to send a card or present to their
god-child on this important anniversary, rather than
observing the child's birthday. In eastern European
homes one often finds the First Communion certificates
of old men and women proudly framed and displayed on
the wall. This relatively small gesture contains even more
poignancy when one considers that many of these
individuals were deprived of Holy Communion for many
years under communist rule. Yet we don't need
persecution to remind us that the day we first received the
Body of Christ was a day our life changed forever.

The number of the sacraments is limited to seven; only
seven material things offer us the possibility of
encountering the Trinity in this most intimate way. The
two sacraments that figure most largely in our ordinary
lives - the Eucharist and Reconciliation - warrant their
own discussion at the end of this section. Yet all the
things that God created were created to draw us to Him.
A life lived sacramentally everyday is a life that
recognises the potential of natural things to provide us a
stepping-stone to God.

Grounding the spiritual in the natural

Indeed, anywhere that we find the True, the Good, and the Beautiful, God is preparing our hearts to be opened to him. As families, we can use this beauty to draw ourselves and our loved ones into greater relationship with God. A greater emphasis on the sacramental meaning of things, sensible beauty, and celebration is an approach especially suited to families, since it allows us to transform everyday life into prayer. Families don't always have the chance to kneel in adoration before the Blessed Sacrament as much as they might like to, but families must be concerned with meals, clothing, the home, sleeping, cleaning and so forth. These material needs can all become meaningful when considered under the aspect of how they bring us into the presence of God.

Deepening the sacramental quality of our lives provides a great entry into the life of prayer because we humans were created as beings that can only come to knowledge through our senses. Sensory experience is the first way that we learn when we are children and the first step in our processes of learning as adults. God planted sensible beauty in his creation in order to draw us corporeal beings along the path to him, the immaterial Beautiful.

The need to involve the senses in interior prayer corresponds to a requirement of our human nature.

We are body and spirit, and we experience the need
to translate our feelings externally. We must pray
with our whole being to give all power possible to
our supplication (*CCC*, 2702).

This understanding of the way humans are constituted
indicates to us that sensible beauty can become a
powerful tool and vehicle in our quest to deepen the
prayer life of our families. If we think about it carefully,
we should all be able to see the power of attraction that
sensible beauty already has for the individuals in our
families. One exciting step towards a deeper prayer life is
to *lay hold of whatever aspects of creation our family
members find beautiful and allow that beauty to lift us up
into greater relationship with the Lord.*

The *spiritual* life of the family must be grounded in the
natural life of the family or it will lack roots, and like the
plant in the parable, it will wither in the sun (*Mt* 13:5). A
family that comes together *only* for prayers may discover
that their communal prayers are characterised by a certain
hollowness or loneliness. Or if a family does not make a
practice ordinarily of sharing meals together, the attempt
to have a meal of religious significance for a special
occasion will fall flat. This happens because community
prayer presupposes a community.

Devotions and customs that are rooted in the local
culture or the personalities of one's own family members

have more of a chance of thriving than customs that have been devised by parents in order to produce a specific religious effect among their children. The practices of another family (or another nation) might be appealing, but it will take thoughtful reflection and experience to discern if they will truly work or will seem artificial with your own family. Moreover, adopting the customs and prayers of your own parish or region have the advantage of uniting in prayer your family with the church and the world at large. After all, families don't exist in isolation, but are themselves part of larger communities.

With family members who are resistant to formal prayer, many times the sacramental approach - drawing near to God through the senses - is the best way to prepare the ground for the Holy Spirit's work of conversion. Teenagers are often thirsting for sensory expression, and just starting to explore their own sense of beauty. But appealing to the senses is also an especially fruitful approach when the family contains small children, because for these little persons who can't yet comprehend the abstract, it speaks to them at the level of the concrete. At the same time it doesn't dilute the faith for them but gives them something real which will grow in meaning as they mature. When we consider each of the senses, we can see how little touches of beauty can offer everyday ways to draw the mind back to God.

Using the five senses

Visual beauty is often the most eloquent way to communicate that our everyday lives are being lived in the presence and Providence of God. Decorating the home differently for various feasts and seasons, wearing special clothes for Sunday or setting the table more beautifully are all simple ways of infusing religious times with a spirit of celebration. Lighting a candle wherever people sit down together is a silent but lovely reminder that Christ is present in this domestic Church. Flowers bring the beauty of God's creation inside; placing them beneath a picture of Our Lady draws the viewer's eye to her, while placing them in living areas announces a special feast. Sanctifying everyday life for children includes gestures as simple as displaying religious pictures or statues of their patron saints in one's home, or reading children's books that recount events from Scripture.

Children respond especially to singing, and music is a particularly powerful way in which earthly beauty can provide a precursor to heavenly beauty. One advantage that hymns have is that their lyrics teach catechetical truths without the potential tedium of dry memorisation. Our two-year-old learned the Latin Gregorian chant *Salve Regina* simply by hearing it at Mass. When we sang "Come Holy Ghost" for Pentecost and the old English carol "The Angel Gabriel" for the feast of the

Annunciation, we were surprised to discover the religious truths that our toddler had absorbed from these songs. We know one family that celebrate the Christmas season by listening together, at the end of every day, to a particularly beloved recording of "For unto us a child is born" from Handel's *Messiah*. Another family observe the same season by singing a Christmas carol chosen by each child at the close of family prayers.

Meals and food might seem the farthest thing from the spiritual life but in fact it's one of the first areas in which prayer can be introduced into one's family; it is no wonder that Christ chose this aspect of human life to become the source and summit of the sacraments. On a very basic, practical level, Grace Before Meals is usually the easiest prayer to form the habit of saying as a family. But meals can bring family members together in many more fundamental ways - we all need to eat! Coming together around a table to share a meal is one of the most formative acts a family can accomplish together - it forges a deep and daily unity. Many of us lament that our families rarely sit down together to share a meal. Perhaps accomplishing this very sacramental act should be among the first goals of a family wishing to grow in love and prayer. A family can begin by sitting down to a special meal every Sunday - with television, computer, iPod, and radio turned off - and as the habit grows stronger it can be extended to weekdays as well.

Aside from its potential for building the culture of the family, a meal can be a liturgical act as well. This meaningfulness was bestowed on food when Jesus gave himself to the Church at a supper with his Apostles under the appearance of bread. At that time he showed us that gathering to eat together could furnish a chance to strengthen our fellowship, and that something as humble and mundane as food could signify for us the highest things. Thus fixing a special meal for a religious occasion can have the two-fold benefit of honouring the occasion and bringing the family together as a community for a shared physical need.

The sense of taste, though it may seem the lowliest of the senses, is in many ways of first importance to young children. Feeding one's children is one of the most basic responsibilities that parents face. But food is not simply a material need but can also be a sign of spiritual meaning. It has been used for centuries to mark the liturgical year - fasting during times of penance or preparation, feasting during festive times, even celebrating particular days with particular special foods, such as the Mediterranean custom of eating cream puffs to celebrate the feast of St. Joseph. Many of us already associate certain foods with certain seasons and feast days. Special foods can play an important role in making certain occasions special. Serving the family's favorite treats during Easter week heightens the sense of an all-out celebration. Fasting on a special bread or Hot Crossed Bun that is reserved for Good Friday preserves the penitential nature of that day while drawing out the unique character and special sweetness of its sacrifice. One Pentecost celebration that we attended featured a dish of nine fruits which sparked a discussion of the nine fruits of the Holy Spirit (*Ga* 5:22).

One very practical advantage to this aspect of sacramentalism is that food speaks to small children in a very dramatic way! Children learn to look forward to a celebratory dish or meal, no matter how simple. One Dutch Catholic, in considering how his parents handed on their faith to him, remembers that after the family members all went to confession, his parents would treat them to small cakes in celebration; the sweetness of those cakes formed a very positive association and happy memory for him.

Yet as we consider ways to involve all the senses in our relationship with God, the impact of silence should not be forgotten. Sitting for a moment in silence at the end of the day, to reflect on our lives and turn our concerns over to God, is an important step on the road to contemplation. While all these forms of sensory input provide us with first entryways into the life of prayer, learning to collect ourselves in silence is a great advancement on that road.

As one father of six described it:

> Lighting a candle and sitting for a moment in
> silence to reflect on the events of the day and to
> bring your needs before God is something you
> could do with almost anyone. It's also a great first
> step towards an examination of conscience. Once
> the family can begin night-time prayers with a
> moment of silence in which each person may
> examine his own conscience, it lays the daily
> groundwork for getting the greatest benefit from the
> sacrament of reconciliation. Meanwhile it prevents
> one's life and habits from slipping by unnoticed.

Reconciliation and the Eucharist

Yet no matter how sacramentally we live our lives, we
will experience a deep lack if we live them without the
sacraments. We owe it to our children to bring them to
these most intense channels of grace by having them
baptised and confirmed. Yet these *sacraments of
initiation* are, as their name implies, only the beginning.
If we want prayer to grow in our families, if we want to
progress in our own spiritual lives, we must live lives
with the sacraments, especially the Eucharist and
Reconciliation, at their centre.

The sacrament of Reconciliation, sometimes referred to as
Confession or Penance, is not simply for transforming one's

soul from a state of mortal sin to a state of grace. The Church teaches that by bringing our venial sins - the petty sins that nevertheless plague all of us - to confession, we receive the grace to overcome them as well. Making honest, searching confessions depends on making honest, regular examinations of conscience. Already by this simple act of observing our thoughts, words, actions, and failures we will make greater progress in becoming better persons. But we will not even have the power to overcome piddling sins without the grace of Christ's passion, which we receive in the sacraments.

No one can compel another person to go to confession, any more than contrition or forgiveness can be forced. Yet we owe it to our children to make it possible for them to receive the sacrament of reconciliation regularly, especially since most children receive this sacrament while still too young to drive. In order to ensure that their family members have the opportunity to go to confession regularly, some families make appointments for individual confessions in conjunction with the devotion to the Sacred Heart of Jesus. According to the message revealed to Saint Margaret Mary Alacoque in the 1670s, twelve special graces are promised to those who honour the Sacred Heart by receiving Communion and Reconciliation on nine consecutive first Fridays of the month. Other families find that choosing a particular confessor to act as spiritual director helps them receive this sacrament with more regularity and fruitfulness.

The Eucharist and the Mass

"The Eucharist contains and expresses all forms of prayer," the catechism proclaims (*CCC*, 2643). That is because it offers us the most perfect union we can have with God on earth - the closest we can come to heaven in this life.

In the context of the Mass, the supreme prayer of the Church, the Eucharist offers us both a highly intimate communion with our Lord, and a liturgical act that unites us with the Church around the world, and all the faithful living and dead. The Mass is the feast that Love invites us to share, and it makes present the sacrifice at which Love "bore the blame" for our sins. There we assist at the death that Love suffered for us, and participate in the life that He lives with us. Mother Teresa promised, "If you really want to grow in love, come back to the Eucharist, come back to that Adoration." Her reason for this was simple: "Unless we have Jesus we cannot give Him; that is why we need the Eucharist."

If any one change could make a drastic difference in a person's spiritual life, a commitment to attending Mass would certainly be the one. Attending Mass every Sunday and Holy Day of Obligation is a law of the Church, and bringing up one's family in the faith must begin there. The Church designates certain days as Holy Days of Obligation because she finds that the graces to be received on those days are so abundant that no one should be without them. To attend Mass as a way of honouring other special days, such as patriotic holidays or family anniversaries, both sanctifies those days and reinforces the celebratory or solemn aspect of Holy Mass in our minds.

Attending daily Mass often calls for real sacrifices of our time, energy, and even sleep. Yet making these sacrifices and ordering our day around the Paschal Sacrifice can make a deep impression on our children (and ourselves!) concerning the gift and privilege that we enjoy at daily Mass. Often this reality is most clearly brought home to us when, after forming a habit of attending daily Mass, we are unable to attend for some reason or another.

Daily Mass can be a great bond and grace for a family. Susie and Michael Waldstein, who have raised eight children in three countries, have been daily Mass-goers for nearly thirty years. The Waldsteins consider that one of the reasons their children never rebelled against attending daily Mass was that it was never treated as an option, but rather practised, calmly and gladly, as a matter of course:

> We have tried to go to daily Mass from the beginning of our marriage. We have brought along all of our eight children as they were born. We have made it a matter of course - part of our life like breakfast, lunch, and dinner. There has seldom been a struggle with a child - a child saying "I don't want to go." It's simply what we do.

Being fed by the Eucharist and slowly growing in it has been a pillar of family life. I cannot imagine surviving twenty-seven years of dishes and housework, ten moves, two babies dying after birth and twenty years of home-schooling without being fed by the Eucharist daily. It is truly our source of life and joy. One of the greatest gifts children bring is the realisation of our absolute neediness. After a too-short night, interrupted several times by nursing, a difficult morning home-schooling and facing the laundry, cooking, and cleaning to do in the afternoon, I have found myself starving for the Eucharist - longing for it from the bottom of my heart and feeling that I could not possibly go on without it. Now that my children are older and I am better organised, my life is easier but I miss that feeling of starving for the Eucharist.

It is difficult to fit Mass in. We have found an early evening Mass to be the easiest. My husband can usually finish work and meet us at Mass. I try to prepare dinner ahead of time or have the meal cooking in the oven during Mass. We have often brought snacks to eat in the car on the way home to prevent hunger crabbiness from souring our drive home. We have also made sandwiches and met my husband at noon Mass and then eaten a picnic lunch with him afterward. This was only possible in the summer in most of the places where we lived. The most important thing is to form a strict routine. It is much easier to go at the same time every day; otherwise it may seem like an option.

When our children have grown up and moved away from home, they have tried to continue daily Mass. One daughter told me that she thought at first that she would only go a couple of times a week because she was so busy but she missed the Eucharist so much that she made up her mind that she needed daily Mass for her whole life.

At times when daily Mass is an impossibility, prayer before the Blessed Sacrament can furnish at least a spiritual communion. Parish workers in America have been amazed at how enthusiastically Eucharistic Adoration is received among teenage students. Many of them have never seen the Eucharist exposed in a monstrance or experienced a Holy Hour, yet when introduced to Adoration they respond as to something that they have been longing for.

The word 'Eucharist' means *thanksgiving*; one way to reflect on this mystery is with the Psalmist who asks, *What return shall I make to the Lord for all the good He has done for me?* The surprising answer is: *I will take the cup of salvation and call upon the name of the Lord.* (*Ps* 116:12) The only thanks that God wants in return for his love and blessings to us is for us to remain in his love, to remain in his grace - to take the cup of salvation that he is extending to us. Nowhere will we find it more tangibly than at Mass, where we witness the sacrifice that continues to save us, and we meet Christ in the Presence that continues to sustain us.

A FINAL WORD

Writing this booklet has been a very humbling experience. Although we never considered ourselves at all qualified to "write the book" on prayer in the family, we consented to do so because we are fortunate to have as examples many faithful Christian families of all sizes and dispositions. What these diverse families hold in common is that they are ambitious to find ways to raise their children in a life of prayer. Speaking to them and observing the practices that they cultivate in their own homes has merely shown us how much more we might do to place Christ at the centre of our family.

At the heart of prayer, whether it takes place in words or through actions, is the recognition of the presence of God with us and the enjoyment of his company. We have learned from parents about their efforts to pray together more as a couple and as a family. We have been moved by their striving to train their own hearts in the truth, to open their minds to the will of God and to search their own consciences for a better way to live. And we have been inspired by all the ways we encountered that mothers and fathers bring themselves into communion with Christ while going about their daily tasks. By increasingly seeking to fill the fabric of their ordinary lives with the awareness of God's presence these families do infuse their lives with prayer - and their lives have a rich, attractive quality because of it.

If you have picked up this book, you probably share our desire for a deeper relationship with Christ and ways to cultivate that relationship in your home. We hope that reading it will help you, as writing it has helped us, to reinvigorate our faith, our families, and ultimately our culture.

Useful Prayers for the Family

An Act of Contrition

O my God, I am sorry for my sins with all my heart. In choosing to do wrong and failing to do good, I have sinned against you whom I should love above all things. I firmly intend to do penance, to sin no more, and to avoid whatever leads me to sin.

Morning Offering

O Jesus, through the Immaculate Heart of Mary, I offer to you all my prayers, works, joys and sufferings of this day, for all the intentions of your Sacred Heart, in union with the holy sacrifice of the Mass throughout the world, in reparation for my sins, and for the intentions of the Holy Father.

Guardian Angel

Angel of God, my guardian dear,
to whom God's love commits me here,
ever this day be at my side
to light and guard, to rule and guide.
From sinful stain, O keep me free,
and at my death my helper be.

The Angelus

1. The Angel of the Lord appeared unto Mary:
2. And she conceived by the Holy Spirit. (*Hail Mary...*)

1. Behold the handmaid of the Lord:
2. Be it done unto me according to your word. (*Hail Mary...*)

1. And the Word was made flesh:
2. And dwelt among us. (*Hail Mary...*)

1. Pray for us, O Holy Mother of God,
2. That we may be made worthy of the promises of Christ.

Let us pray. Pour forth, we beseech thee, O Lord, thy grace into our hearts, that we to whom the Incarnation of Christ thy Son was made known by the message of an angel, may by his Passion and Cross be brought to the glory of his resurrection. Through the same Christ our Lord. Amen.

Grace Before Meals

Bless us, O Lord, and these thy gifts, which we are about to receive from thy bounty, through Christ our Lord. Amen.

Grace After Meals

We give thee thanks, Almighty God, for these and all thy benefits, who lives and reigns forever. Amen.

Further Resources

Catechism of the Catholic Church. (Continuum, 2000)

Compendium: Catechism of the Catholic Church. (Catholic Truth Society, 2006) Question-and-answer format to the catechism.

Familiaris Consortio: Apostolic Exhortation on the Role of the Christian Family in the Modern World. Pope John Paul II. (CTS, 1982) The papal encyclical on the role of the family.

Rosarium Virginis Mariae: Apostolic Letter on the Most Holy Rosary (CTS, 2002): John Paul II discusses the structure and significance of the Rosary, while offering some practical suggestions for making it more meaningful to the individual.

The Rosary of Pope John Paul II: The 20 Mysteries, (Libreria Editrice Vaticana, Vatican City: Vatican Press, 2002). Each mystery of the Rosary is accompanied by a beautiful work of art and a meditation from Scripture and the Catechism.

Scriptural Rosary: A Modern Version of the Way the Rosary was Once Prayed Throughout Western Europe in the Late Middle Ages. (Christianica, 1989) This tiny book gives a relevant line of Scripture to mediate on for each Hail Mary.

Shorter Morning and Evening Prayer. (2006). An abbreviated form of the liturgy of the hours, suitable for praying in the family.

Book of Feasts and Seasons. Joanna Bogle (Gracewing, 1992) Gives suggestions for ways to commemorate the various times of the liturgical and natural year in the family.

A Continual Feast: A Cookbook to Celebrate the Joys of Family and Faith Throughout the Christian Year. Evelyn BirgeWitz (Ignatius Press, 1991). A cookbook which follows the course of the liturgical year, offering recipes for special occasions.

Around the Year with the Trapp Family Singers. Maria Von Trapp. The famous Austrian mother describes family customs for celebrating the liturgical year.

Handbook of Christian Feasts and Customs. Fr. Francis X. Weiser (Harcourt, 1958). A more scholarly, historical explanation for the development of various Christian customs from around the world.

Splendor in the Ordinary: Your Home as a Holy Place. Thomas Howard. (Sophia Institute Press, 2001) A consideration of the deeper spiritual meaning of the places in one's home. Also published under the title *Hallowed be this House.*

Introduction to the Devout Life. St. Francis de Sales. (Bantam, Doubleday, Dell; 1990) In this spiritual classic, a doctor of the church and bishop gives basic instruction in prayer for the average layman.

The Story of a Soul: The Autobiography of St. Theresa of Lisieux. St. Therese Martin. (TAN Books and Publishers, U.S.: 1997). A doctor of the church and cloistered nun explains her "Little Way" of doing daily activities as acts of love.

Saint Gianna Molla: Wife, Mother, Doctor. Pietro Molla and Elio Guerriero. (Ignatius Press, 2004). An interview with the husband of the Italian laywoman who was canonized in 2004.
The Story of a Family: the Home of St. Therese of Lisieux. Fr. Stephane Piat. (TAN Books and Publishers, 1994). A study of the family that produced five religious sisters and at least one saint.

The Good Shepherd and the Child: A Joyful Journey. Cavalletti, Gobbi, Coulter, and Montanara. (Liturgy Training Publications, 1994). An introduction to Good Shepherd Catechesis, which uses Montessori principles to help children learn to pray.
The Religious Potential of the Child: Experiencing Scripture and Liturgy with Young Children. Sofia Cavaletti. (Liturgy Training Publications, 1993). Scripture professor and founder of Good Shepherd Catechesis shares insights she has gained from her work with children.

(Magisterial documents, including the catechism, council documents, apostolic letters, and encyclicals, may be found online by visiting www.vatican.va and clicking on "The Holy See" and "Papal Archive" for papal documents or "Resource Library" for catechism, Vatican II and Canon Law.)

Informative Catholic Reading

We hope that you have enjoyed reading this booklet.

If you would like to find out more about CTS booklets - we'll send you our free information pack and catalogue.

Please send us your details:

Name ....

Address ....

....

....

Postcode ....

Telephone..

Email ....

Send to: CTS, 40-46 Harleyford Road,
            Vauxhall, London
            SE11 5AY

Tel: 020 7640 0042
Fax: 020 7640 0046
Email: info@cts-online.org.uk

 **CTS**